The Extraordinary SUZY WRIGHT

A Colonial Woman on the Frontier

Teri Kanefield

ABRAMS BOOKS FOR YOUNG READERS · NEW YORK

PREVIOUS PAGE: Quaker women rarely sat for full-color portraits, believing that doing so was vain and extravagant. The technique of making a portrait by sketching a silhouette, however, was deemed acceptable. There is no known image of Suzy Wright, but if she had allowed her portrait to be done, it would most likely have been a silhouette, like this one of Sally Norris, granddaughter to Isaac Norris and a friend of Suzy's, c. 1800. Artist unknown.

For Joel, who shared the journey

Cataloging-in-Publication Data has been applied for and may be obtained from the Library of Congress.

ISBN: 978-1-4197-1866-3

Text copyright © 2016 Teri Kanefield
For image credits, see page 62.
Book design by Maria T. Middleton

Printed and bound in China
10 9 8 7 6 5 4 3 2 1

Abrams Books for Young Readers are available at special discounts when purchased in quantity for premiums and promotions as well as fundraising or educational use. Special editions can also be created to specification. For details, contact specialsales@abramsbooks.com or the address below.

THE ART OF BOOKS SINCE 1949

115 West 18th Street
New York, NY 10011
www.abramsbooks.com

CONTENTS

SUZY COMES TO AMERICA

Ships in Distress in a Storm, c. 1720–1730, by Peter Monamy. The painting captures the dangers of ocean crossings at the time that Suzy and her family journeyed from England to the colonies.

cean crossings were dangerous in the year 1714, when sixteen-year-old Susanna Wright—called Suzy by friends and family—sailed with her family from England to the American colonies. Their ship met with violent storms. One time, the rocking was so severe that Suzy was thrown from her bed. Another time, the ship rolled so far that the end of a mast submerged in the

water and came loose. The space below the main deck flooded, and everyone inside—including Suzy—was soaked.

Suzy was traveling with her parents, John and Patience, and her younger siblings, twelve-year-old Eleanor, eight-year-old Patience, and four-year-old John. Her mother was expecting another child.

Back in England, Suzy's family had lived in a large, well-furnished house in Lancashire. Her father and uncles were successful cloth merchants known as linen drapers. They bought and sold luxury fabrics, laces, buttons, and other trimmings. The Wrights were also members of a group persecuted in England, the Religious Society of Friends. Members of this group were also called Quakers, because they were said to tremble in the presence of the Lord. In addition to being a merchant, Suzy's father was a Quaker minister.

Like others before them and many others to come, Suzy and her family were leaving their home and all that was familiar in search of religious freedom. They planned to make their new home in the colony of Pennsylvania.

An engraving of High Street, Chelmsford, England, c. mid-1700s, by J. Ryland, showing a view that would have been similar to towns in Lancashire at the time.

An illustration depicting a Quaker persecution in England, c. late 1600s. Artist unknown.

QUAKERS

For Quakers, the words "friend" and "Quaker" are synonymous. Their religious gatherings are called meetings. Their places of gathering are called meeting houses. Among other things, Quakers believe in equality for all people. They are pacifists, opposing all forms of violence, including war. They value integrity and simplicity.

Quakers in England in the 1700s were persecuted partly because they rejected many of the teachings and requirements of the Church of England. The Quakers' belief that all people were equal directly challenged the social order in England, which placed lords and ladies—and of course the king—above common people. Quaker loyalty to the monarchy was thus questioned. Quakers were also seen as potential traitors because they didn't believe in signing oaths of loyalty, so they refused to sign their allegiance to the Crown.

Suzy's maternal grandfather, a Quaker minister, had been fined and beaten for his beliefs. By the time Suzy, her parents, and her siblings were on their way to the New World, the worst of the persecutions were past. Still, Quakers in England were discriminated against, harassed, and generally not trusted by non-Quakers.

Upon arriving at the mouth of the Delaware River, Suzy and her family sailed to the port of Philadelphia, where they were greeted warmly by the Quaker community. Suzy felt at home right away, surrounded by people who shared her beliefs and values:

It is indeed a charming city and country—more friends than other people in it and 2 great meeting houses.

—SUZY TO HER COUSIN WILLIAM CROUDSON, JULY 1, 1714

Suzy concluded her first recorded letter written in the colony of Pennsylvania with these words:

I often think of all my relations and friends left in England, but can't think of seeing England anymore. The pleasantness of this country and the toil of the sea journey will hinder me. I must once more bid you farewell, but hope not forever. Your truly loving cousin, though at this distance—you in one quarter of the world and I in another.

Pennsylvania

New Jersey

Maryland

TOP: A map of the colony of Pennsylvania and the other mid-Atlantic British colonies, 1776.

BOTTOM: A view of Philadelphia from the New Jersey shore, 1768.

7

AT HOME IN THE LAND OF BROTHERLY LOVE

The first Chester Meeting House, built in 1693. Suzy and her family became members shortly after their arrival in Pennsylvania. Date and artist unknown.

he Wrights' new home stood on more than two hundred acres in Chester County, just west of Philadelphia along the Delaware River. They joined the Chester Meeting. On November 19, 1714, five months after their arrival, Suzy's youngest brother, James, was born. Within a few years, Suzy's father became justice of the peace for Chester County and was elected to the Pennsylvania General Assembly.

PENN'S WOODS

The colony of Pennsylvania was founded by and for Quakers. In 1681, King Charles of England gave the land to William Penn, a Quaker, to repay a debt. The king may have had another motive as well. Allowing Penn to start a Quaker colony in the New World got many of the most troublesome Quakers—those freethinkers with upsetting ideas—out of England.

William Penn wanted his colony to be a "holy experiment," a place of peace and freedom. So under English law, the land was his; the English way of thinking was that the Indians didn't count. The first thing Penn did upon arriving, though, was purchase parts of Pennsylvania from the Indians and work to create close friendships so the Indians and colonists could share the land. He believed that respecting Indian customs and dealing with the Indians fairly would insure peace.

Because Penn envisioned perpetual peace, he wanted a colony without forts or a militia. In 1701, when he drew up the Charter of Privileges, or basic laws of the land, he made sure that all people, whatever their religion, would have the freedom to worship as they pleased. That wasn't all. He made sure that nobody would be imprisoned without a jury trial, and he created light punishments for crimes. Instead of jails, he created temporary workhouses. He set up a system that allowed disputes to be resolved among the citizens without formal courts.

The colony would be ruled by a governor and two legislative branches, the Provincial Council and the General Assembly, frequently simply called the Assembly. The Assembly was the larger, more representative branch of government.

Penn named his colony Pennsylvania, which means "Penn's woods." He named the capital of his colony Philadelphia, which means "brotherly love."

Flagmen of Lowestoft: Admiral Sir William Penn, 1665–1666, by Peter Lely. This portrait was painted about fifteen years prior to King Charles bequeathing Penn the land in the New World.

The Treaty of Penn with the Indians, 1771–1772, by Benjamin West. The actual peace treaty was reportedly signed in October 1682 near the village of Shackamaxon, in what is now Kensington, Pennsylvania.

Suzy was, by all accounts, likable, an engaging conversationalist, and brilliant. She loved books and learning. She read Italian and Latin and spoke French, and she

was uncommonly agreeable in conversation, and indeed was equalled by few, and her letters were highly deservedly admired. Her character throughout was excellent. . . . [She had received] a good education according to its estimation at that time, but the high degree of culture which her mind afterwards attained was entirely owing to her own diligence and love of literature.

—DEBORAH NORRIS LOGAN, QUAKER AND GRANDDAUGHTER TO ISAAC NORRIS, 1815

TOP: *James Logan*, c. 1716, by Gustavus Hesselius.
BOTTOM: Isaac Norris, c. 1750. Artist unknown.

Suzy soon earned the admiration and friendship of the colony's leaders—men many years older than she. She became close friends with James Logan, who was then chief justice of the colony and would later become mayor of Philadelphia and, finally, acting governor. James Logan, like Suzy, enjoyed reading and discussing philosophy and ideas. He was a classics scholar with a knowledge of Latin, Greek, Hebrew, and Arabic. Suzy and Logan shared an interest in literature and philosophy.

Also among Suzy's early friends was Isaac Norris, a prominent councilman and member of the Assembly. Isaac Norris also liked languages. He was fluent in French, Latin, and Hebrew, and he owned one of the most extensive libraries in the colonies. He and James Logan frequently lent Suzy books and discussed ideas with her.

The respect Suzy earned as a very young woman from such men as James Logan and Isaac Norris tells us much about her. Not only could she hold her own in an intellectual discussion with the most educated members of the community, but the leaders of the colony sought her company, enjoyed her conversation, and respected her ideas.

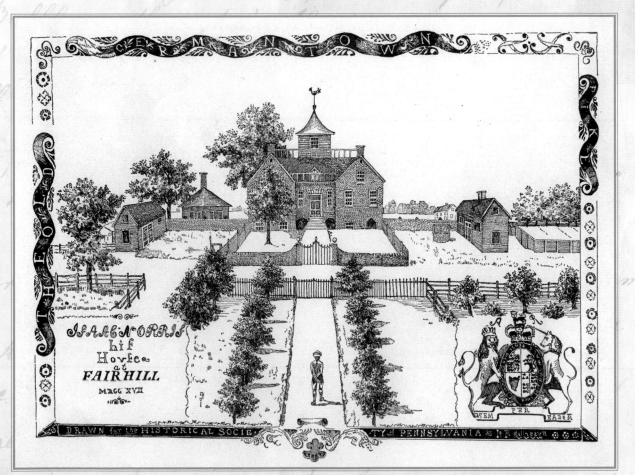

Fairhill, the home of Isaac Norris, built in 1717, on the outskirts of Philadelphia. Date and artist unknown.

Sarah, James Logan's daughter, c. 1750. Artist unknown. Sarah was born in 1715, shortly after Suzy's family arrived in America. Later she married Isaac Norris's son, Isaac Norris Jr.

Suzy remained friends with the Logan and Norris families for the rest of her life. She eventually befriended their children and grandchildren, including Deborah Logan, granddaughter to Isaac Norris who, after Suzy's death, wrote a detailed account of her personality and accomplishments. As she said later of the friendships she formed upon first arriving in Pennsylvania:

The first intimacies I contracted, and the happiest hours I ever enjoyed since I left my native land were in [Isaac Norris's] house. The strongest friendships I formed there were only dissolved by death, which must sooner or later break every human tie.

—SUZY WRIGHT TO POET AND FELLOW QUAKER HANNAH GRIFFITTS, APRIL 5, 1762

SHAKING OFF THE YOKE

Weak woman, thus in agreement grown strong
Shakes off the yoke her parents wore too long

—SUZY WRIGHT

 amuel Blunston, a well-to-do Philadelphia Quaker eight years older than Suzy, was a surveyor by profession. Samuel—we are told by Elizabeth Hiestand, a descendant of one of Suzy's sisters—fell in love with Suzy and wanted to marry her:

> *[The] affection . . . was fully reciprocated, but by an unfortunate train of circumstances, loves affairs went awry and they never married.*

According to another source, Samuel Blunston was "a suitor for the hand of Susanna, who refused him several times."

Because Suzy wouldn't marry Samuel, he instead married a widow, Sarah Bilton.

Suzy never married. The account given by Elizabeth Hiestand does not tell why "loves affairs" between Suzy and Samuel went awry, but historians looking for reasons had to search no further than Suzy's feelings about men and marriage.

Quakers Meeting, c. late 1600s, by Egbert van Heemskerck the Elder. The Quakers' belief that women were equal to men meant that Quaker women had more freedom than women in other groups. Quaker women could even be ministers. This drawing shows a Quaker woman speaking in a religious meeting.

Suzy strove to live her life according to Quaker ideals, and a cornerstone of the Quaker faith was that *all* people—including women—were equal. The idea that men and women were equal was a radical one in the eighteenth century. Under colonial law, as in England, men were considered superior. Women could not run for public office or vote. Once a woman married, her husband had complete control of her property—and of her. A single woman, on the other hand, could own her own property and do many other things a man could do, such as enter legal agreements, appear in court on her own behalf, and decide what she wanted written in her will.

Because—according to Quaker ideals—the souls of men and women were equal, Suzy opposed the laws governing marriage; she believed a man had no right to control a woman.

She cautioned women not to fall for the "soft soothing flattery" of men, which would lead to "wearing the chain."

Colonial women who remained single were often ridiculed for their choice. The Puritans of New England, for example, believed that for a woman not to become a wife and mother was "not simply odd, but deviant." But in the much more tolerant colony of Pennsylvania, a woman such as Suzy was able to remain single while retaining the respect of her community.

Later, a few younger Quaker women followed her lead. Hannah Griffitts, thirty years younger than Suzy, became Suzy's friend and correspondent. Hannah said she chose to remain single to "keep my dear liberty as long as I can."

. . . .

Thus Suzy enjoyed her life as an unmarried woman in the comforts of Chester County, not far from Philadelphia, where she had access to the best libraries in the colony, the respect of the governing elite, and friends who shared her interests and beliefs.

Then, in 1726, tragedy struck: Suzy's mother died. Suzy assumed the responsibility of caring for her younger brothers and sisters, particularly the youngest, James, who was then twelve. She remained an "authority in the family" all her life. After raising James and her younger sisters, she presided over the upbringing of nieces and nephews.

Around the time Suzy's mother died, James Logan, who was then serving as chief justice of the colony, proposed that a Quaker settlement be established on the frontier, which then ran along the Susquehanna River about seventy miles west of Philadelphia. The word "frontier" comes from the French word meaning "borderland," the region of a country that "fronts" on another country. In North America, the frontier was the line between the areas settled by Europeans and the lands to the west.

Quaker tolerance for all people—particularly the Quaker policy of allowing religious freedom—made Pennsylvania attractive to non-Quaker settlers as well. Unfortunately, many of these non-Quakers behaved lawlessly, taking lands that belonged to the Indians and generally making trouble. Logan wanted a Quaker settlement on the frontier to keep the peace and spread Quaker ideals.

A land dispute between Maryland and Pennsylvania added to the unrest on the frontier.

Maryland claimed that its boundaries extended north into the lands claimed by Pennsylvania. So another reason Logan wanted a settlement of Pennsylvanians on the banks of the Susquehanna was to reinforce Pennsylvania's claim to the land.

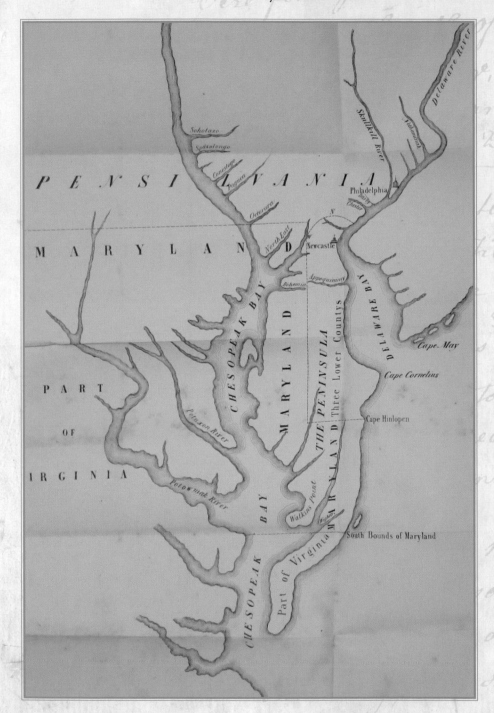

This map shows the boundary between Maryland and Pennsylvania.

In addition to serving as chief justice for the colony, Logan was the personal agent for the Penn family, who were then in England. He was thus one of the most powerful citizens of the colony, with authority to dispense land on the frontier. He selected a few Quakers he trusted to found the new settlement: the Wrights, Samuel Blunston and his wife, Sarah, and a third settler, Robert Barber, whose oldest daughter later married Suzy's brother John. One historian suggested that Logan chose the Wrights partly because of "his unique friendship and regard for a remarkable woman many years his junior, Susanna Wright."

Suzy's father, John Wright, was the first pioneer to visit the area. In 1726 he journeyed seventy miles west through the wilderness to the Susquehanna River area. He familiarized himself with the land and befriended local Indians, whose nearby village consisted of two or three dozen Indian huts.

Suzy was the first member of her

family to buy land on the frontier—which she could do as an unmarried woman. On August 31, 1726, when she was twenty-eight, she bought one hundred acres adjoining the Susquehanna River. Two weeks later, her father bought 150 acres neighboring hers, and they made their plans to head west. Samuel Blunston purchased a neighboring parcel to the north. Robert Barber bought lands to the south.

Isaac Norris, who had recently completed his term as mayor of Philadelphia, told Suzy that her task in going to the frontier was to:

propagate civility, good sense, reason, and good manners, and to propagate moral justice.

—ISAAC NORRIS TO SUZY WRIGHT, APRIL 18, 1728

Promoting and spreading moral justice—particularly on the frontier—was a tall order. Suzy, as she later proved, was up to the task.

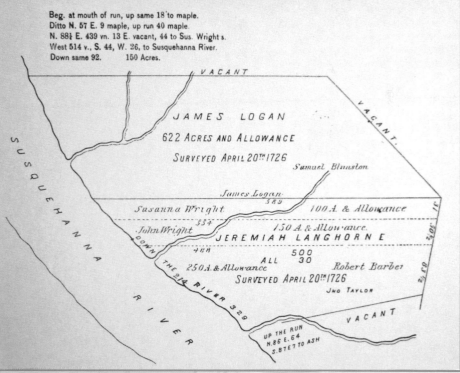

TOP: The Susquehannock people, also called the Conestogas by the English, lived along the Susquehanna River and the region stretching from the south part of what is now New York through central Pennsylvania and as far south as Virginia. This detail is taken from *John's Smith's Map of the Chesapeake Bay*, c. 1608.

BOTTOM: A survey drawing showing the Wright and Blunston landholdings. Year unknown.

A NEW HOME ON THE FRONTIER

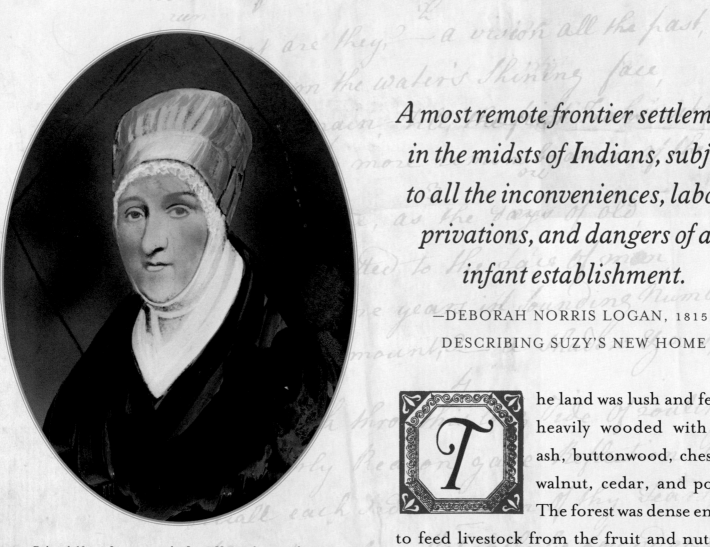

Deborah Norris Logan, c. early 1800s. Year and artist unknown.

A most remote frontier settlement, in the midsts of Indians, subject to all the inconveniences, labors, privations, and dangers of an infant establishment.

—DEBORAH NORRIS LOGAN, 1815, DESCRIBING SUZY'S NEW HOME

he land was lush and fertile, heavily wooded with oak, ash, buttonwood, chestnut, walnut, cedar, and poplar. The forest was dense enough to feed livestock from the fruit and nuts that grew wild there. The river was wide, calm, and majestic. Suzy's property—like her father's and

Susquehanna River today, looking out from Suzy's property.

Samuel Blunston's—reached down a gently sloping hill to the riverfront, along a stretch where the water was slow moving and shallow. A small stream ran through Samuel's property, where he later built a sawmill.

Despite the rustic beauty of her new home, a poem Suzy wrote shortly after arriving on the frontier sums up her feelings about being out in the wilds:

From all the social world estrang'd
in desert wilds and woods
Books and engaging friends exchanged
For pendant rocks and floods

As was common for settlers first arriving on the frontier, Suzy's family and the other pioneers who joined them built log cabins. The idea was to build a simple shelter as a short-term home until a more permanent and finer structure could be built. The first cabin the Wrights built was a log house on John's property, about a hundred yards from the river's edge. The house was built from white-oak logs and at first contained only a single room for the entire family.

Suzy's life on the frontier meant hard labor from morning to evening, with Suzy and her family working alongside hired and indentured servants (see sidebar on page 25):

Reconstructed log cabin similar to what the Wrights would have built when they first settled on the frontier. The simple construction and meager interior greatly contrasts the luxurious homes like those of Isaac Norris outside Philadelphia.

Reconstructed log-cabin interior. Suzy's first home would have been furnished in a similar way.

Each morning dawn to labor calls
Through noontide's sultry sun
And when the dew of evening falls,
The task is but begun.

Suzy missed Philadelphia and her friends there, where life had been easier, but she understood that she had to accept the lot given to her:

Ah! how unlike those days of peace
By earlier prospects given!
But hush, my heart, thy murmurs cease,
And take thy lot from heaven.

Petition for the Establishment of Lancaster County, signed February 6, 1729. The petition listed arguments in favor of forming a new county: The region was too heavily populated to be administered effectively from Chester; because of the distance, the "arm of justice" was weakened; and travel to and from the courthouse was expensive and time-consuming.

At the same time, she appreciated the beauty of the land and the charm of a rustic life so far from the city:

Behold the trees their leaves spume
The shrubs and herbage rise
Unbidden flowers the groves perfume
And all serene the skies.

Behold the morn and evening sun
The rock and waterfall,
Retract the wrong that thou hast done
To scenes that never pall.

Within two years, Samuel Blunston was the first of the settlers to complete construction on a stone house, a two-story structure with a curved staircase and a basement. Suzy's sisters were both married in Blunston's newly built house on the same day, June 5, 1728. Eleanor and her husband settled on the frontier not far away, while Patience and her husband returned to Chester County.

Shortly afterward, John Wright, Samuel Blunston, and Robert Barber petitioned the deputy governor, Patrick Gordon, and the Assembly to form a new county. When, in 1729, their county was approved, they named it Lancaster for the Wrights' native Lancashire in England. John Wright was the first justice of the peace for the newly formed county. Hickory Town, a community about ten miles to the east with a population of about two hundred, was the new county's largest and most populated community, and was later renamed the town of Lancaster.

Soon other settlers came to the area. Because "a lawless element was a plague to the settlers of the area," a functioning court was badly needed. Samuel Blunston was the first clerk of the court. There was no courthouse, so the legal work and court business was done in his house. Suzy served as Samuel's assistant—settling estates, issuing patents, and hearing the complaints of the Indians and others. In Blunston's office was a window, and:

to this little office window came the litigants of that time. Here were brought the wills for probate, here were brought the deeds and patents for record. . . . To this window came the noble red man to seek relief from the grasping, and oppressive white settler.

Blunston was not trained as a lawyer and, by all accounts, Suzy was better educated. Thus, they were more likely equal partners. In fact, Suzy was often instrumental in getting court business done. James Logan, who was then serving as chief justice for the entire colony of Pennsylvania, sent Suzy—not Samuel Blunston—a letter explaining that until their local court ordered the road Logan wanted, he would not grant Suzy's father permission to operate a ferry. James Logan wrote to Suzy because he knew that he could depend upon her:

He [John Weems] observed to me that I might have a greater dependence on thy friendship for me in this case than on all the court besides. I request you at your next ensuing court to press it on your father and Samuel Blunston that when a road is ordered, but not before, I shall easily obtain grant of a ferry.

—JAMES LOGAN TO SUZY WRIGHT, MARCH 24, UNKNOWN YEAR

By 1730, a road connecting the town of Lancaster to the Wrights' settlement was built, and sure enough, John Wright received a grant to operate a ferry. The boats were made from hollowed-out tree trunks large enough to carry more than a ton. The water was shallow enough for the boats to be pulled by animals from one side to the other. Suzy's brother John built a tavern for travelers on the west side of the river. John Wright senior and junior operated the ferry with the help of German indentured servants.

Trouble between Pennsylvania and Maryland heated up when a number of Marylanders came to the area, took land from the Indians without paying for it, and burned their homes. John Wright sent a letter to the deputy governor of Pennsylvania, Patrick Gordon, explaining that:

A Ferry Scene on the Susquehanna at Wright's Ferry, near Havre de Grace, 1787–1839, by Pavel Petrovich Svinin.

A person who wished to come to the colonies but could not afford passage often agreed to work as a servant for a fixed number of years in exchange for boat fare. The servant received room and board but no payment and had very little personal freedom. After working for the agreed-upon term, the servant was released from the contract. This was called indentured servitude.

An example of an indentured contract between a Patrick Larkin and Thomas Blood, dated August 17, 1766. Under the terms of the contract, Thomas Blood agreed to pay Patrick Larkin's passage to America and food and lodging for a seven-year period, during which time Patrick agreed to work as a servant. At the end of the term, Thomas consented to pay him a cash settlement and end his bondage to the contract.

people of loose morals and turbulent spirits came and disturbed the Indians—our friends and allies—who were peaceably settled on these lands ... burnt their cabins and destroyed their goods and with much threatening and ill-usage, drove them away. ... Thus they proceeded to play booty, disturbing the peace of the government, carrying people out of the province by violence, taking away the guns from our friends the Indians, tying and making them prisoners without any offense given, and threatening all who should oppose them.

The Marylanders' view of the situation was that the land in question belonged to Maryland and that the Pennsylvania settlers were squatters. The leader of the Marylanders, Thomas Cresap, was an infamous frontiersman and, in the view of the Pennsylvanians, a "blustering bully." He built a fort not far from the Wrights' settlements and made it his goal to rid the Susquehanna valley of the Pennsylvanians and the Indians. He made forays into Pennsylvanian settlements, destroying homes and taking property, on the theory that the settlers owed taxes to the colony of Maryland. More than once, he and bands of Marylanders trampled the Wrights' lands.

Sporadic violence continued for several years. In 1735, while Suzy's father and some of his workers were in the fields, Cresap approached with twenty heavily armed people, including women and children. They carried swords and pistols and beat drums. John Wright confronted them and demanded an explanation. Cresap said that he and his fellow Marylanders had come to fight the Pennsylvanians.

John Wright stood his ground. Cresap, expecting the passive Quakers to be easier to intimidate, retreated. He returned with a small militia provided by the governor of Maryland. When the Pennsylvanians felt they had exhausted all means of keeping the peace, Samuel Smith, the Lancaster County sheriff, decided to charge Cresap with the murder of a Pennsylvanian, deputy sheriff Knowles Daunt. Smith issued a warrant for Cresap's arrest.

Deciding to arrest a lawless ruffian such as Cresap was one thing. Succeeding was another.

On the night of November 23, 1736, Sheriff Samuel Smith and twenty-four armed non-Quakers surrounded Cresap's house and set it on fire. When Cresap fled the burning building, the Pennsylvanians captured him, took him to the Lancaster town workhouse, and put him in irons. They later transferred him to a prison in Philadelphia. While being paraded through the streets of Philadelphia, Cresap, with his usual defiant spirit, looked around and said, "This is the prettiest town in Maryland!"

Even with Cresap in prison, Marylanders continued their attempts to dislodge the Pennsylvanians. The two colonies eventually petitioned the king of England for help. In response, a royal committee organized negotiations. On May 25, 1738, the colonial leaders signed an agreement allowing for an exchange of prisoners and a renewed boundary fifteen miles south of Philadelphia, thus ending what came to be known as Cresap's War. Thomas Cresap later held a position in the Maryland government and died a wealthy landowner.

· · · · · · · · · ·

Despite six years of upsets from Cresap and other Marylanders, the Wrights' ferry prospered, providing an income for the family and turning the settlement into a crossroads, strategically situated beside a major waterway and crossing point to the western territory. At times, demand for the ferry was so great that travelers with their wagons had to wait more than a day for their turn.

Income from the ferry allowed the Wright family to build more permanent homes, including a two-story stone house on the land Suzy owned. The labor, like the labor used to run the ferry, was provided by indentured servants and hired workers.

Suzy's house, where she and her brother James lived, had a parlor and a kitchen downstairs, two bedrooms and a small office upstairs, and a basement for storage. She planted and tended lush apple orchards and amassed a library of several hundred books in multiple languages.

The settlement came to be called Wright's Ferry.

Suzy's house as it looks today, after having been restored by the current owners. When the house was newly built by Suzy and situated on the frontier, it would not have been landscaped in this manner.

A LITTLE
ROMANCE

n addition to her orchards, Suzy cultivated a garden, where she grew medicinal herbs. She distributed the medicines to the Indians and settlers in need. When Samuel Blunston's wife, Sarah, grew ill, Suzy tended to her and corresponded with a Philadelphia doctor about the medications she needed and the best ways to treat her.

Sarah died in 1744. After her death, Samuel and Suzy rekindled their romance. When, several years later, Samuel fell ill, Suzy tended to him as she had tended to Sarah. During Samuel's final illness, she managed all his household and personal business and official court duties.

Samuel's will caused a stir because he left Suzy money and property in the exact same way a man left money and property to his wife under what was called a "dowager portion." He left Suzy a sizable income from his estate, the freedom to use and profit from his lands, and the use of his house and property during her lifetime. Because Samuel's will allowed Suzy a dowager portion, historians have concluded that he and Suzy had a romantic relationship.

This romance, in the words of Elizabeth Hiestand, "brightened and softened" Samuel's final years, allowing him time with the woman he first loved in a life that would otherwise have been given over entirely to "tough battlings with a new settlement, border ruffianism, and other great responsibilities."

POLITICAL ADVISER, LAWYER, ACTIVIST, AND ADVOCATE FOR THE INDIANS

She was well known and generally esteemed by the most eminent characters in the state of Pennsylvania.... I had the pleasure, when I was very young, of seeing her, and can remember something of the vivacity and spirit of her conversation, which I have since heard some of the best judges of such merit affirm they had seldom known to be equaled.

—DEBORAH NORRIS LOGAN, 1815

I n popular imagination, folklore, and legend, the American frontier was a land of lawlessness and gunfights, cowboys and Indians, and wide-open spaces. Although there was indeed a measure of lawlessness, the frontier was also a place of opportunity for women. Often there were not enough capable men to do work generally considered for men only, so an intelligent and competent woman could simply step in and do what needed to be done. Similarly, such professions as law were not regulated. Those smart enough to read law books and figure out how to draw up contracts could do it.

Some historical accounts claim that after Samuel's death, Suzy became the court clerk. Others say that, as a woman, she could not have had an official appointment. The most likely explanation is that, on the frontier, legal proceedings were conducted casually, so Suzy was treated as a court official and acted as one without formal appointment. When settlers in the vicinity of Wright's Ferry had disagreements over land or how to handle a will or some other matter, they turned to Suzy, the most bookish and intellectual settler in the area. She drafted wills and legal documents for her less literate neighbors. She advised Indians about land matters, and she settled disputes.

A surviving letter Suzy wrote in 1776 to the chief justice of the court in Lancaster shows that she represented the legal interests of her family in the Lancaster County court, and she even gave the chief justice, Jasper Yeates, instructions:

An orphans court will be desired to meet on Monday next, to appoint guardians for the children of my late dear brother; for which purpose, his Eldest son & our relation Robert Barber will wait upon you early in the day in hopes of having it completed before night, as there is no settlement than merely appointing guardians, the persons who are desired, are John Dickinson, whose permission to be named one of them, he sent us in writing. . . .

I am so particular as you may perhaps have leisure before Monday to prepare any necessary writing with more convenience, than you could do in an hour's warning.

—SUZY WRIGHT TO JASPER YEATES, JANUARY 18, 1776

The letter Suzy wrote to Chief Justice Jasper Yeates in 1776.

By the early 1740s, the population of Lancaster County had grown considerably. Suzy's father passed away in 1749. His oldest daughter was, by then, a force in the county. During one hotly contested election for the Pennsylvania Assembly, Suzy knew which candidate she wanted to win. She wrote a pamphlet designed to arouse the passions of anyone reading it, sent a copy to every congregation in the county, and used her influence to make sure it was read widely in Quaker meetings.

As if that wasn't enough, she stood in an upper room in a tavern in the town of Lancaster and, all through election day, distributed copies of her pamphlet from the window.

Her candidate won. The failed candidate blamed Suzy for his defeat:

Could anyone believe that Suzy could act so unbecoming and unfemale a part as to be employed in copying such infamous stuff and to take her stand as she did at Lancaster in an Upper Room in a public house and to have a ladder erected to the window and there distribute lies and tickets all the day of the elections?

The outpouring of emotion in the letter quoted above makes clear that the candidate targeted by Suzy's leaflet was outraged by her behavior. Women were not supposed to interfere in politics.

As one of Suzy's nieces reportedly said, "Woe betide to anyone who went against Aunt Suzy."

....

Although there is no record of when or where Suzy Wright and Benjamin Franklin first became acquainted, surviving letters indicate that by the 1740s, Franklin was a frequent visitor to Suzy's home in Wright's Ferry, and that by the early 1750s a warm friendship had developed between them:

When I had the pleasure of seeing you, I mentioned a new kind of candle very convenient to read by, which I think you said you had not seen. I take the freedom to send you a specimen of them. . . . Accept an Almanac for the New Year with my hearty wishes that it may prove a happy one to you and your friends.

—BENJAMIN FRANKLIN
TO SUZY WRIGHT,
NOVEMBER 21, 1751

Benjamin Franklin, 1706–1790, by David Martin, 1767.

We have had excessive hot weather now near two weeks. My thermometer has been almost every day at 94, and 95, and once at 97, which is but 3 degrees short of the hot Sunday June 18, 1749. [Philadelphia] is a mere oven. How happily situated are our friends at [Wright's Ferry]. I languish for the country, for air and shade and leisure, but fate has doomed me to be stifled and roasted and teased to death in a city. You should not regret the want of city conversation if you considered that 9/10ths of it is impertinence.

—BENJAMIN FRANKLIN TO SUZY WRIGHT, JULY 11, 1752

Franklin sent Suzy pamphlets and essays, lent her books, and discussed religion and ideas with her. Suzy also corresponded regularly with Franklin's wife, Deborah Read Franklin, and daughter, Sarah "Sally" Franklin Bache. While the correspondence between the women was warm and intimate, it is unknown whether they ever met in person. Their friendship appears to have originated entirely through Benjamin Franklin. In one exchange of letters, Deborah Franklin tells Suzy her fears about one of her husband's ocean crossings.

When Benjamin Franklin—one of America's most eminent statesmen—needed something done in Philadelphia, he knew how to achieve it. He understood the culture and politics, the personalities and the quirks of Philadelphia and other major cities. When he needed something done on the Pennsylvania frontier, he called on Suzy.

In 1755, the French and Indian War was in full swing. The British and French were fighting over control of the colonies. The French strategy was to recruit local Indians and turn them against the British. It appeared to be working. As the war moved toward Pennsylvania, other

Deborah Read Franklin, Benjamin Franklin's wife, corresponded with Suzy and considered her a friend, c. 1758. Attributed to Benjamin Wilson.

Sarah Franklin Bache, by John Hoppner, 1793. Franklin's daughter, Sally, also corresponded with Suzy. It appears that Suzy's friendship with both Sally and Deborah came about through her friendship with Benjamin Franklin.

colonies expected the worst: Nobody trusted that the pacifist Quakers who ruled Pennsylvania would be able to support an army. How could they be depended on to defend their citizens in the face of an attack, when fighting was against their religion and beliefs?

British general Edward Braddock and his army were en route from Maryland to Fort Duquesne, in what is now Pittsburgh. His mission: to take Fort Duquesne from the French. The governors of Maryland and Virginia promised that, when he reached Fort Cumberland in Maryland, 250 wagons for transport would be waiting for him. He arrived to find fewer than twenty.

General Edward Braddock (1695–1755), the British officer and commander-in-chief in the French and Indian War whose troops were awaiting transport wagons from the colonies, c. nineteenth century. Artist unknown.

The British soldiers cursed the colonials for being dishonorable and dishonest. The Virginians and Marylanders blamed the Quakers of Pennsylvania for failing to supply the remaining wagons.

The Pennsylvania Assembly sent Benjamin Franklin to visit General Braddock and "remove the prejudices the General was understood to hold against the Quaker government in Pennsylvania." Among Franklin's tasks was to round up enough horses and wagons so the British soldiers could march with their supplies across the Allegheny Mountains to take Fort Duquesne.

Franklin knew that all the farmers in Lancaster had wagons. He had money from General Braddock to pay for them, but, given how spread out the farms were across Lancaster, he didn't know how to gather so many in a short time. He visited Wright's Ferry and met with Suzy and her brother James.

A few days later it was Suzy whom he thanked for the idea he used—with some modifications:

Dear Madam,
I thought from the first, that your proposal of calling the several townships together, was very judicious. I was only at a loss how to get them called by some appearance of authority. On the road from your house, I considered that at the Court of Oyer and Terminer here, there would probably be constables from most of the townships, and if the Chief Justice could be prevailed on to recommend it from the Bench, that the constables should immediately call the Inhabitants of their respective Townships together, perhaps the Business might by that means be effectually done....

—BENJAMIN FRANKLIN TO SUZY WRIGHT, APRIL 28, 1755

A copy of one of Benjamin Franklin's letters to Suzy, sent April 28, 1755.

The idea evidently worked. Franklin got the word to the various townships and succeeded in gathering 150 wagons and 262 horses. It is unclear from surviving letters how Suzy reconciled the gathering of army supplies with her Quaker beliefs. Presumably Suzy struggled with the same issue as the Quaker leaders in Pennsylvania: How could a Quaker reconcile the ideals of pacifism with the requirements of government, which included protecting citizens?

Not long afterward, the Wrights helped Benjamin Franklin out of another tight spot. Braddock's soldiers needed additional flour, and the General Assembly called upon Franklin to figure out how to obtain it. On April 27, 1755, Suzy understood that if the soldiers met with any misfortune, "whatever cause it may be owing, it will be attributed to their march being hindered for the want of this flour." James Wright therefore agreed to furnish the necessary flour from his mill.

Despite having enough wagons and flour, General Braddock was defeated. The result was chaos and fear on the Pennsylvania frontier. The settlers near Wright's Ferry, terrified of an attack by the

In the fall of 1755, after Braddock's defeat, the inhabitants of Wright's Ferry feared for their safety, so they fortified this house owned by John Wright on the west side of the Susquehanna River, because it was considered the most secure structure in the area, c. 1850. Artist unknown.

French and their Indian allies, selected what they considered the strongest building in the area—a stone house owned by Suzy's brother John on the west bank of the Susquehanna River—and fortified it to withstand an attack.

But the danger passed. The war never came to Wright's Ferry.

....

Suzy was a protector and advocate for the Indians. After a series of attacks on the Indians, she wrote a passionate letter to a prominent member of the Pennsylvania Assembly begging for their protection. After a group of non-Quakers brutally murdered a peaceful band of Conestogas, she contributed, with Benjamin Franklin, to a fiery and eloquent pamphlet denouncing the massacre and arousing sympathy for the Indians, whom she called "friends of this Province."

Suzy took such an interest in Indian affairs that many years later, a Lancaster assemblyman wrote to Joseph Reed—a Pennsylvania politician who served as a delegate to the Continental Congress and signed the Articles of Confederation—telling him that if he wanted to know the history of the Pennsylvania land disputes with the Indians, he should seek out Suzy Wright, who could give him a full account.

A

NARRATIVE

OF THE LATE

MASSACRES,

IN

LANCASTER COUNTY,

OF A

Number of *INDIANS*,

FRIENDS of this PROVINCE,

By PERSONS Unknown.

With some *Observations* on the same.

Printed in the Year M,DCC,LXIV.

This twenty-three-page pamphlet published in 1764 was long attributed to Benjamin Franklin. Scholars have recently concluded that Suzy was at least a coauthor.

BUSINESSWOMAN AND SCIENTIFIC AUTHOR

Silkworms.

n the latter part of the eighteenth century, Benjamin Franklin and other colonial leaders encouraged the founding of a local silk industry, which they saw as potentially lucrative and as a way of establishing colonial autonomy. Suzy, by then past her seventieth birthday, responded by learning to raise silkworms and make silk, defying the expectations of age just as she had al-

ways defied the expectations of gender. She thus became one of the first women in the colonies to operate a business, following the career path her father, uncles, and grandfather pursued as linen drapers in England.

She did most of the work herself. In spring, she fed the silkworms with mulberry leaves, covered them with linen, and tucked them into a drawer so they could spin their cocoons. She then placed the cocoons in boiling water and skimmed the floating silk filaments, which she wound onto a spindle and then washed until they were soft and ready for spinning.

> *As early as 1770, Susanna Wright made a piece of mantua [a heavy weave of silk] of sixty yards length, from her own cocoons, of which I have preserved some specimens. . . .*
>
> —JOHN F. WATSON, HISTORIAN, 1830

In 1771, a society was formed in Philadelphia to encourage the production of silk in the colonies. The society petitioned the legislature for premiums to be offered to those who could produce silk in large quantities. First prize went to Suzy.

Her silk skeins were sent to England, where they were woven into cloth. When Benjamin Franklin visited the royal court in England in the 1770s, he presented a dress made of Suzy's silk to Queen Charlotte that the queen promised to wear for the king's birthday celebrations.

Historian Robert Proud visited Suzy in 1772, when she was seventy-five years old, and reported that there were 1,500 silkworms at their labor "under the charge of the celebrated Susanna Wright." Suzy told Proud that, with a little encouragement, she could have one million silkworms busily producing silk.

After becoming an expert in how to raise silkworms and produce silk, Suzy wrote a scientific article entitled "Directions for the Management of Silkworms," which was published after her death in the *Philadelphia Medical and Physical Journal*, possibly making Suzy the first American woman to author a scholarly scientific article.

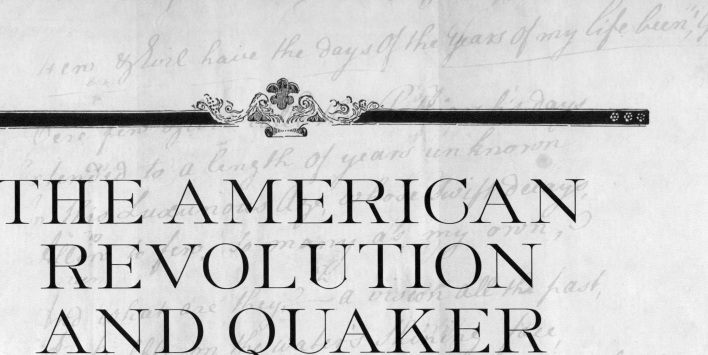

THE AMERICAN REVOLUTION AND QUAKER PACIFISM

The French and Indian War left the British in debt. To relieve that debt, the British imposed special taxes on the colonies. Many colonists—angry about the taxes—wanted independence from England. They demanded war.

As war become more likely, Quakers argued among themselves and wrestled with their own consciences about how much they could support a revolutionary war while remaining true to their ideals of peace and nonviolence. Many of the Quakers in the Pennsylvania Assembly resigned because they could not—in good conscience—prepare for war. Some Quakers remained, arguing that it was wiser to bend their beliefs and maintain their power. James Wright, Suzy's youngest brother, who had initially joined the Assembly at her urging, resigned his Assembly seat in 1771.

Suzy was seventy-nine years old in 1776 when America declared its independence.

Once the war got under way, Suzy's surviving letters make it clear that she despised the British soldiers and their actions. When the British marched into Philadelphia and occupied the city, she called them "bandits" and "miscreants with no spark of honor," and she believed that all citizens should flee the city at once:

Why would not every person who had it in their power,
leave that devoted city, before those miscreants entered it?
I can in no way account for the conduct of several individuals,
who might have come to places of more probable security—
but now have only to wish they had done it.

—SUZY WRIGHT TO HANNAH THOMSON, WIFE OF CHARLES THOMSON,
ONE OF THE PATRIOT LEADERS IN PHILADELPHIA AND LATER SECRETARY
OF THE CONTINENTAL CONGRESS, 1777

Her sympathy with the revolutionaries was shown through her lively and friendly correspondence with prominent non-Quakers who ardently supported the war. Having helped Benjamin Franklin solve his wagons-and-flour crisis, she obviously found it acceptable under her religious beliefs to provide material support to soldiers. She also most likely supported the general Quaker position that peaceful protests—such as fighting unfair British taxation by boycotting British goods—were preferable to war. When confronted with aggression—as in the case of the murder of Indians—she wanted "these violent men opposed and the defenseless people protected."

Yet Suzy appears to have drawn the line at picking up a weapon in the cause of independence and revolution. When she learned that one of her nephews, John Lowdon, had gone to visit the troops, she wrote a letter telling him not to get any ideas about joining the fighting. Theirs was a "family of peace," and she had no intention of allowing any member of her family to pick up arms:

DISCRIMINATION AGAINST QUAKERS

During the American Revolution, many Quakers found themselves the victims of discrimination and harassment because their pacifist beliefs kept them from supporting war and signing writs of allegiance. As a result, they were seen as unpatriotic and untrustworthy. The backlash against the Quakers for their pacifist views during the Revolutionary War was reminiscent of the discrimination that caused them to leave England in the first place.

We were much surprised at the news of your present expedition and can by no means approve of it, if your design is other than to visit the camp of our brave countrymen and satisfy your own curiosity, and then return, as other gentlemen from this province will, I presume, wisely do.... But I hope and trust you will reflect and not be carried away with an inordinate military enthusiasm to get yourself shot through the head when you really have no call to it.

—SUZY WRIGHT TO HER NEPHEW, JOHN LOWDON, JULY 18, 1775

She could only bend her ideals of peace and non-violence so far. Although she could condone the use of violence to protect the innocent, she could not allow a member of her family to pick up arms and join a war—even a war fought to rid the colonies of "miscreants with no spark of honor."

CELEBRATED POET

She was indeed the most literary lady of the province . . .

—JOHN F. WATSON, HISTORIAN, 1830

uzy was part of a circle of prolific poets, a group of women who corresponded and exchanged their poems. Although the poetry of women in general was not taken seriously by the literary establishment in the eighteenth century, female Quaker teachers often promoted the work of women writers by assigning their poems to students for copying. For example, in 1763, two Quakers, Rebecca Jones and Hannah Catherall, began what would be a successful twenty-year teaching career when they founded a school in Philadelphia for both boys and girls. It was patronized by many of the elite families of the city. The two teachers frequently used Suzy's poems as part of their lessons.

Several of Suzy's philosophical poems were written

The text of Suzy's poem "My Own Birthday," 1761, survives in Suzy's own handwriting.

Until the end of the twentieth century, only four of Suzy's poems were known to have survived, two because they were published after her death in literary journals. Then in 1997, another twenty-four of her poems were discovered in a long-forgotten "commonplace" book—a blank book in which one of Suzy's contemporaries, Milcah Martha Moore, had copied poems she particularly admired. Pictured here is Suzy's poem "On Time" as it appeared in Moore's book.

On Time. —————— *by the same*

Since Moments past are as a Dream,
    A fleeting Evening Shade,
Which close like a divided Stream
    Like dying Tapers fade. ——
Enjoy the Present & be blessd,
    While yet they're in yr. Power,
Nor Place yr. Happiness or Rest,
    In any future Hour.
But know the Present will be gone
    And leave the Soul no more,
To feed its craving Wishes on,
    Than what you now deplore;
Enjoy the Present, but secure,
    The future as you go;
Alone the Future must endure
    A Happiness or Woe.
It will be present in its Time,
    But never can be passd
To an eternal Now you climb
    Which must forever last. ——

as part of her correspondence with James Logan. In her poetry she wrote about such topics as human happiness, knowledge, and power.

One of her most accomplished poems, "The Grove," tells of a beautiful grove, the home of a peaceful philosopher, that was destroyed by war and greed. "The Grove" can be read as Suzy's commentary on the fate of Pennsylvania—"Penn's Woods"—the Quaker experiment where people could live freely and in peace. The Quaker dream of perfect peace, like the grove in Suzy's poem, was destroyed by human greed, war, and "turbulent spirits."

LAST YEARS
AND LEGACY

y the late 1770s, the American frontier had moved westward. Daniel Boone blazed a trail from Virginia into central Kentucky. Settlers poured westward into what is now Ohio. Although it was no longer a frontier settlement, Wright's Ferry remained sparsely populated and rural.

Into her eighties, Suzy, from her home in Wright's Ferry, continued writing letters and poems, tending to the poor in her community, and exerting her influence in the highest political and literary circles. She was eighty-six years old when she was visited by the noted physician and politician Benjamin Rush, who recorded in his journal:

Benjamin Rush, in an engraving from 1800. Artist unknown.

47

I saw the famous Suzy Wright, a lady
who has been celebrated above half a
century for her good wit, good sense, and
valuable improvements of the mind.
She has been for many years the friend
and correspondent of Dr. Franklin. . . .

—BENJAMIN RUSH, 1784

Suzy was declining in strength, but she still took delight in her books, declaring to Benjamin Rush that she could not do without them.

She died later that year, on December 1, 1784. In accordance with the Quaker custom based on rejecting personal vanity, she was buried in an unmarked grave.

. . . .

Piecing together the details of Suzy's life is—in the words of one historian—like putting together a jigsaw puzzle with most of the pieces missing. Only about thirty of her letters survive, even though she was a prolific letter writer all her life and had a great many correspondents, including statesmen and politicians at the highest levels of government. Because so much has been lost, and because women were often overlooked by historians, we may never know the full extent of her influence.

It is clear, though, from surviving letters and legal documents, that Suzy thrived on the frontier. Living there as a single woman and landowner gave her independence and autonomy, allowing her to step into roles forbidden to women in towns and cities and more settled areas.

As an unmarried woman, she enjoyed many of the same personal liberties as men in her social class. Leaders of the colony kept her informed and sought her advice. She generously used her talents for the betterment of her community. She never sought personal recognition, but she achieved fame during her lifetime through the power of her intellect, her personality, and her compassion.

The following lines were written in the year 1726, by *Susannah Wright*, on removing from Chester County to the banks of the Susquehanna—the spot where the Town of Columbia now stands. The writer was the ancestor of the respectable family of that name who now reside in Columbia.

From all the social world estrang'd,
  In desert wilds and woods,
Books and engaging friends exchang'd
  For pendant rocks and floods;

Nature's uncultivated face
  A varying aspect wears;
But every charm and every grace
  Are sunk in stronger cares.

Each morning dawn to labour calls,
  Through noontide's sultry sun,
And when the dew of ev'ning falls,
  The task is but begun.

Lamps (wont to guide calm midnight hours
  O'er the amusing page,
Of poetry th' enchanting pow'rs,
  The wisdom of the sage,)

Now gild the midnight hours of toil,
  'Till weary nature fails,
'Till glimmering they have spent their oil,
  And balmy sleep prevails;

'Till morning dawn renews the day,
  And with the day its care;
So pass the hours of life away
  Through the unvarying year.

Ah! how unlike those days of peace
  By earlier prospects given!
But hush, my heart, thy murmurs cease,
  And take thy lot from Heaven.

With spirit act thy painful part,
  Subdue thy erring will,
Thy passions regulate, thy heart
  Guard from each thought of ill.

Then shall thy waning hours of day,
  (If life such hours shall bring,)
Pass like a cloudless eve away
  To an eternal spring.

Meantime enjoy this season fair,
  And every joy that's given,
Shake from thy mind the weight of care,
  And bless indulgent heaven.

Behold the trees their leaves resume,
  The shrubs and herbage rise,
Unbidden flowers the groves perfume,
  And all serene the skies.

Behold the morn and evening sun,
  The rock and water-fall,
Retract the wrong that thou hast done
  To scenes that never pall;

A scene the hand of nature drew
  With all-surpassing skill,
Keeps through a thousand ages new
  Its pristine glories still.

The morning sun revives and warms,
  In native splendour bright,
And evening soft, with wonted charms,
  Leads on the shades of night.

The moon as pure her beams can shed,
  And stars as brightly glow,
As when you arch of heaven was spread
  First o'er this world below.

Behold the morn and evening sun,
  The rock and water-fall,
Retract the wrong that thou hast done
  To scenes that never pall.

Suzy's poem "From All the Social World Estrang'd," 1726, written shortly after she moved to the frontier and published after her death in the *Literary Magazine and American Register, Vol. II*, Philadelphia, June 1804.

AFTERWORD

FROM WRIGHT'S FERRY TO COLUMBIA

Suzy left her house and all her land to her nephew, Samuel, son of her youngest brother, James. To draw citizens to Wright's Ferry and found an actual town, Samuel had the land he inherited from Suzy surveyed and laid out in 160-acre lots, which he distributed through a lottery. As a result, the population grew.

Samuel had high ambitions. The new United States government was then searching for a site for the capital, and he worked to have his town adopted, arguing that its strategic location on a major waterway at a crossroads to the open frontier out west made the location ideal.

Samuel changed the name of the town from Wright's Ferry to Columbia, believing a patriotic name might help the town's chances of being selected. When a vote was taken for the site of the new capital, Columbia, Pennsylvania, lost by a single vote. Residents of Columbia maintain that the name given to the capital of the United States—Washington, the District of *Columbia*—got its inspiration from the name Samuel Wright gave to their town.

HOW THE QUAKERS HELPED SHAPE AMERICA

When Suzy arrived in Philadelphia, the majority of its inhabitants were Quakers. By the close of the eighteenth century, Friends still comprised almost a third of the population of Pennsylvania.

Philadelphia, the center of Quaker influence during the eighteenth century, has been called the birthplace of America. By the time of the Revolution, Philadelphia had surpassed Boston as the busiest port in the colonies and the second busiest in the entire British Empire, second only to London. Philadelphia, because of its central location, hosted the First Continental Congress before the war and the Second Continental Congress after. The Declaration of Independence was signed in Philadelphia. Philadelphia served as the temporary capital of the United States while Washington, D.C., was under construction.

The Liberty Bell, an important relic of American patriotism, was a Quaker bell: It was initially ordered in 1751 by Isaac Norris Jr. and a few other Pennsylvania officials to commemorate the

The Liberty Bell.

fiftieth anniversary of William Penn's 1701 Charter of Privileges. Long before the American Revolution, the Quakers inscribed onto the bell the words "Proclaim Liberty throughout all the land unto all the inhabitants thereof."

QUAKERS AS ABOLITIONISTS

Quakers contributed much more to the shaping of America's ideals and values than producing a bell and being early advocates of religious freedom and tolerance. They were among the first and most zealous abolitionists committed to ending slavery. Through much of the seventeenth and eighteenth centuries, a small percentage of Quakers owned slaves, believing the practice was acceptable as long as the slaves were treated according to Quaker ideals. By the mid-1770s, however, Quakers uniformly rejected slavery as incompatible with their beliefs about equality for all people.

Quakers were instrumental in helping to run the Underground Railroad. According to accounts from those who were alive when the Underground Railroad operated, the stone house Suzy's brother James built for her on her property later became a "well-known station on the Underground Railroad."

Quakers took a leading role in providing stopping places for runaway slaves along the Underground Railroad. For example, Levi Coffin, a Quaker, was often called the President of the Underground Railroad, and the home he shared with his wife, Catherine, pictured here, was nicknamed Grand Central Station because thousands of escaped slaves passed through.

When segregation was in full swing in the South and black children were denied equal education, Quakers built and ran schools for them.

Quakers also worked for equal rights for women. As Suzy eloquently explained in her poetry, Quaker ideals of equality for all people meant that women must have rights equal to those of men.

Quakers to this day remain opposed to war, urging peaceful and nonviolent solutions to conflicts and seeking equality for all people everywhere.

As Douglas Gwyn, a Quaker historian, said of the Quakers in Pennsylvania:

They came to do good
And they did very well.

TOP: After the Civil War, Quakers were active in establishing and running schools for freed slaves. This is a photograph of Quaker teachers in the Freedmen's School in Norfolk, Virginia, 1863.

BOTTOM: This drawing from an 1886 newspaper shows a Freedmen's School classroom in Richmond, Virginia.

AUTHOR'S NOTE

I have always been interested in women who refuse to accept the limitations placed on them because of their gender. In the eighteenth century, women were generally believed to be less intelligent than men, ruled by their emotions rather than by reason, so they were seen as unfit for public roles and responsibility. Partly for these reasons, they were not allowed to vote.

I became interested in Suzy Wright while researching the history of female lawyers in early America. Unsurprisingly, there were not many. Legal work was directly opposed to traditional female roles: Lawyers were officers of the court and were expected to speak in public and to think and argue analytically. Historians consider Suzy Wright to be America's second female lawyer—using the term loosely, of course, because the profession was not regulated. The first, a Maryland woman named Margaret Brent (c. 1601–c. 1671), like Suzy, played an important role in the history of her colony.

Researching this book brought me back to Pennsylvania, which I hadn't visited since college graduation. With my ten-year-old son, Joel, I traveled through the state, visiting museums, libraries, and historical societies. We stopped first at the Penn State campus, where I found a 1982 master's thesis about Suzy by Barbara Hunsberger. The thesis was invaluable, because the current owners of Suzy's home are refusing scholars access to the archives containing letters and other documents.

Luckily, Hunsberger had been given access and was able to quote at length all the pertinent letters and documents in the house archives. These documents illustrate Suzy's involvement in politics and public life. They make clear that, although Quaker women had more freedom and a better education than many other groups in the colonies, Suzy nonetheless held an unusual place in her community's politics, culture, and society.

While they do not permit guests to view the letters and other documents in the archives of Suzy's home, the current owners have restored her house, furnished it with a lovely collection of period pieces, and opened it to the public for special tours. Joel and I were able to tour the house, including the cellar, and imagine what it must have been like to live there in the eighteenth century.

We stood on the banks of the Susquehanna and absorbed the quiet loveliness of the river. Gazing westward, we could imagine the region when it was wilderness and the farthest reach of the American frontier.

We visited the Landis Valley Village and Farm Museum in Lancaster County, where we were able to see and photograph the kind of log cabin Suzy would have lived in when she first arrived on the frontier. At the Columbia Historic Preservation Society, the Lancaster Historical Society, and the Historical Society of Pennsylvania, we were permitted to look through all the archives, including original letters, Suzy's handwritten poems, portraits of many of Suzy's contemporaries, and legal documents.

The more I learned about Suzy, the more I found to admire—from her love of books to her hatred of violence. I discovered in her life and ideals a new look at our nation's beginnings.

Notes

As was common in the eighteenth century, Suzy's name was spelled various ways during her lifetime. Her full name was spelled Susannah, Susana, and Susanna. Suzy was occasionally spelled Susie and Suzey. She wrote her own name as Susannah in her will. In the family Bible, her name is spelled Susannah when listing her birth, and Susana when listing her death. However, because her name occurs most often as Susanna and Suzy in the scholarly works I have consulted, those are the forms adopted in this book. For consistency, I have changed the spelling to Susanna and Suzy regardless of how they appear in the original texts. Where I have changed the spelling from the original, there is an endnote.

Further, "Indian" is used to describe the indigenous peoples of the Americas during Suzy's life. As her contempraries used this term, my editor and I made the decision to use "Indian" throughout, instead of "Native American," to avoid confusion.

SUZY COMES TO AMERICA

Page 6: *"It is indeed a charming city."* Throughout the book I modernized the spelling and punctuation in letters to make them more accessible to young readers. I also modernized the spelling in some of the more difficult poems.

AT HOME IN THE LAND OF BROTHERLY LOVE

Page 10: *"was uncommonly agreeable."* Deborah Logan's account was written in 1815 and reprinted in *Hazard's Register of Pennsylvania,* and it has been much quoted by historians. Deborah Logan, who was much younger, met Suzy once and was well acquainted with many of Suzy's close friends and confidants. Much of Logan's narrative is corroborated by original sources. There are also inaccuracies. For example, Logan tells us that Suzy remained in England when her parents and siblings came to Pennsylvania and that she joined her family in the colonies a few years later. This "fact" has been repeated widely and still appears in many scholarly accounts. A letter of Suzy's, however, dated July 15, 1714, shows that, in fact, Suzy came to the American colonies at the same time as her family.

SHAKING OFF THE YOKE

Page 13: *"[The] affection."* Elizabeth Hiestand's account, 32. In approximately 1900, Elizabeth Hiestand, a descendant of Suzy's sister, wrote the stories about Suzy that her grandfather (born 1797) had told her, stories that had been told to him by his older relatives who knew Susanna personally. Stories passed down through the generations can never have the authority of firsthand accounts written at the time, but much of what Hiestand wrote has been verified by sources written while Suzy was alive or shortly after her death. For example, although the romance of Samuel Blunston and Suzy comes largely from family lore, scholars have concluded from Samuel's will that their relationship must have been romantic. Because the family lore was corroborated by scholars, I have given credit to it.

Page 13: *"a suitor for the hand of Susanna* [spelled "Susannah" in the quoted text]*"* Wharton, *In Old Pennsylvania Towns,* 107.

Page 15: *"soft soothing flattery."* Suzy Wright, "To Eliza Norris—at Fairhill" (1750).

Page 15: *"not simply odd, but deviant."* Wulf, *My Dear Liberty,* 85.

Page 15: *"keep my dear liberty."* Hannah Griffitts, "To Sophoronia. In answer to some Lines she directed to be wrote on my fan," 1769, in Blecki and Wulf, *Milcah Martha Moore's Book.*

Page 15: *"authority in the family."* Hiestand, 9.

Page 16: *"his unique friendship."* Blecki and Trese, "Susanna Wright's 'The Grove,'" 239.

A NEW HOME ON THE FRONTIER

Page 18: *"A most remote frontier settlement."* Deborah Logan's account, 1815, reprinted in *Hazard's Register of Pennsylvania.*

Pages 19, 21, 22: *"From all the social world estrang'd."* Suzy Wright, untitled poem (1726).

Page 22: *Eleanor and her husband settled.* Linn, *Annals of Buffalo Valley, Pennsylvania.*

Page 23: *"A lawless element."* Hunsberger, 7.

Page 23: *"to this little office window."* Hiestand, 30.

Page 23: *"He [John Weems] observed to me."* Hunsberger dates the letter 1738/9, but because the ferry was established in 1730, the letter must have predated 1730.

Page 25: *"people of loose morals."* As quoted by Egle, *Illustrated History,* 822.

Page 25: *"blustering bully."* Day, Historical Collections of the State of Pennsylvania, 693.

Page 26: *"This is the prettiest town."* High, *The C&O Canal Companion,* 10.

A LITTLE ROMANCE

Page 28: *"tough battlings with a new settlement."* Hiestand, 32.

POLITICAL ADVISER, LAWYER, ACTIVIST, AND ADVOCATE FOR THE INDIANS

Page 29: *"She was well known."* Deborah Logan's account, 1815, reprinted in *Hazard's Register of Pennsylvania*.

Page 30: *"In that early time."* Wharton, *In Old Pennsylvania Towns*, 105.

Page 32: *"Could anyone believe."* As quoted by Morgan, *Inventing the People*, 193, and *Women and Freedom in Early America*.

Page 32: *"Woe betide to anyone."* Reported by Hiestand.

Page 36: *"remove the prejudices."* Bell and Labaree, "Franklin and the Wagon Affair, 1755," 553.

Page 38: *"whatever cause it may be owing."* Copy of letter on file at the Historical Society of Pennsylvania, Pemberton Papers. As quoted by Hunsberger, 27.

Page 39: *seek out Suzy Wright.* "Dr. Benjamin Rush's Journal of a Trip to Carlisle in 1784," as quoted in Wulf, *Not All Wives*, 194.

BUSINESSWOMAN AND SCIENTIFIC AUTHOR

Page 41: *"As early as 1770, Susanna Wright."* Watson, *Annals of Philadelphia and Pennsylvania in the Olden Time*, 437.

Page 41: *"under the charge of the celebrated Susanna Wright."* As quoted by Watson, *Annals of Philadelphia and Pennsylvania in the Olden Time*, 438.

LAST YEARS AND LEGACY

Page 48: *jigsaw puzzle.* Hunsberger, 3.

AFTERWORD

Page 50: *lost by a single vote.* The Columbia Historic Preservation Society, author site visit and interview with Suzanne Whallon, June 26, 2014.

Page 52: *"well-known station on the Underground Railroad."* Glenn Banner, as quoted by Suzanne Whallon, Vice President of the Columbia Historic Preservation Society, author interview, June 26, 2014.

Page 53: *"They came to do good."* Gwyn, *Seekers Found*, 341–42. While the original source of this quotation appears to be anonymous, Douglas Gwyn analyzed and explained it.

Bibliography

ORIGINAL SOURCES

Original sources include letters, poems, legal documents, and dates written in a family Bible. Susanna Wright's extant correspondence and poetry are at the Historical Society of Pennsylvania, Haverford College, the Chester County (PA) Historical Society, Ferry Mansion archives, and National Archives. Although the current owners of Suzy's house, which they call the Ferry Mansion, are currently denying scholars access to the letters, many of them were quoted by Barbara Hunsberger in her 1982 master's thesis.

Susanna Wright's last will and testament is located in Book E, 160, at the Historical Society of Pennsylvania, Philadelphia.

A bibliography of Susanna Wright's correspondence housed in the public archives is on file at the Lancaster County Historical Society, Lancaster, Pennsylvania.

MANUSCRIPTS

Elizabeth Hiestand's manuscript, written in the early 1900s. A copy is on file at the Columbia Historical Society, Columbia, Pennsylvania.

JOURNAL ENTRIES

"Dr. Benjamin Rush's Journal of a Trip to Carlisle in 1784." As reprinted by Lyman H. Butterfield in *The Pennsylvania Magazine of History and Biography* 74 (Oct. 1950).

BOOKS

Biddle, Gertrude Bosler, and Sarah Dickinson Lowrie, eds. *Notable Women of Pennsylvania*, Committee of 1926 Philadelphia Sesquicentennial Celebration. Philadelphia: University of Pennsylvania Press, 1942.

Blecki, Catherine L., and Karin Wulf, eds. *Milcah Martha Moore's Book: The Commonplace Book of an Eighteenth-Century Woman*. University Park, PA: Pennsylvania State University Press, 1997. Contains the largest extant collection of Susanna Wright's poetry.

Day, Sherman. *Historical Collections of the State of Pennsylvania: A Copious Selection of the Most Interesting Facts, Traditions, Biographical Sketches, Anecdotes, Etc.* Philadelphia: G. W. Gorton, 1843.

Egle, William H., MD. *Illustrated History of the Commonwealth of Pennsylvania: Civil, Political, and*

Military, from Its Earliest Settlement to the Present Time. Harrisburg, PA: De Witt C. Goodrich, 1877.

Ellis, Franklin, and Samuel Evans. *History of Lancaster County, Pennsylvania: With Biographical Sketches of Many of Its Pioneers and Prominent Men.* Philadelphia: Everts & Peck, 1883. Pages 539–42 outline the land purchases and holdings of Susanna and her family.

Gwyn, Douglas. *Seekers Found: Atonement in Early Quaker Experience.* Wallingford, PA: Pendle Hill, 2000.

High, Mike. *The C&O Canal Companion.* Baltimore: Johns Hopkins University Press, 2001.

Hymowitz, Carol, and Michaele Weissman. *A History of Women in America.* New York: Bantam Books, 1978. This supports the thesis that the frontier was a place where women could realize their full potential because there was less division between women's work and men's work.

Knapp, Samuel L. *Female Biography: Containing Notices of Distinguished Women in Different Nations and Ages.* Philadelphia: Thomas Wardle, 1846.

Laulder, Paul, ed. *Heath Anthology of American Literature,* 5th ed. Independence, KY: Cengage Learning, 2008.

Linn, John Blair. *Annals of Buffalo Valley.* Harrisburg, PA: Lane S. Hart, 1877.

Morgan, Edward. *Inventing the People: The Rise of Popular Sovereignty in England and America.* New York: Norton, 1988.

Sage, Lorna. *Cambridge Guide to Women's Writing in English.* New York: Cambridge University Press, 1999. This states that Susanna Wright was "one of the most celebrated writers of her day."

Schaefer, Elizabeth Meg. *Wright's Ferry Mansion: Volume 1: The House.* Darby, PA: Diane Publishing, 2005. This volume about the house, restored as a museum, reveals the history of the house at Wright's Ferry and its original owner, Susanna Wright. Although "the von Hess Foundation has done a splendid job approximating the house's original furnishings with a rich display of regional and historical decorative arts . . . scholars have found it difficult if not impossible to place Susanna Wright intimately in her home. With little documentary evidence and fewer material objects to authenticate her daily life at Wright's Ferry, preservationists have relied on educated guesswork." Stabile, *Memory's Daughters,* 61.

Smith, John, and Gilbert Cope. *History of Chester County, Pennsylvania, with Genealogical and Bibliographical Sketches.* Philadelphia: Louis H. Everts, 1881.

Stabile, Susan M. *Memory's Daughters: The Material Culture of Remembrance in Eighteenth-Century America.* Ithaca, NY: Cornell University Press, 2004.

Stranahan, Susan Q. *Susquehanna, River of Dreams.* Baltimore, MD: The Johns Hopkins University

Press, 1993. This history of the Susquehanna River region provides background on the politics of the Quakers who settled there and devotes five pages to Susanna's life, including her relationship with the local Indians, her legal work, and her friendship with Benjamin Franklin.

Watson, John F. *Annals of Philadelphia and Pennsylvania in the Olden Time; Being a Collection of Memoirs, Anecdotes, and Incidents of the City and its Inhabitants.* Philadelphia: John Penington and Uriah Hunt, 1830.

Wharton, Anne Hollingsworth. *In Old Pennsylvania Towns.* Philadelphia: J.B. Lippincott Company, 1920.

Wulf, Karin. *Not All Wives: Women of Colonial Philadelphia.* Philadelphia: University of Pennsylvania Press, 2005. This looks at Susanna Wright's ideas of equality and why she never married, set in the context of her Quakerism.

ARTICLES

Bell, Whitfield J., and Leonard W. Labaree. "Franklin and the 'Wagon Affair,' 1755." *Proceedings of the American Philosophical Society* 101 (1957): 553.

Blecki, Catherine L., and Lorett Trese. "Susanna Wright's 'The Grove,' A Philosophical Exchange with James Logan." *Early American Literature* 38, no. 2 (2003): 239–55.

Cowell, Pattie. "Wright, Susanna." Mark C. Carnes and John Garraty, eds. *American National Biography* 24 (1999): 59–61.

Doutrich, Paul. "Cresap's War: Expansion and Conflict in the Susquehanna Valley." *Pennsylvania History* 52, no. 2 (April 1986). University Park, PA: Penn State University Press.

Hazard, Samuel, ed. "Some Account of the Early Poets and Poetry of Pennsylvania." *Hazard's Register of Pennsylvania: Devoted to the Preservation of Facts and Documents and Every Other Kind of Useful Information Respecting the State of Pennsylvania* 12, no. 194 (Sept. 17, 1831): 177–78.

Reninger, Marion Wallace. "Susanna Wright." *Journal of the Lancaster County Historical Society* 63, no. 4 (October 1959): 183–90.

Shirk, Willias L., Jr. "Wright's Ferry: A Glimpse into the Susquehanna Backcountry." *Pennsylvania Magazine of History and Biography* CXX, nos. 1/2 (January/April 1996).

Wright, Susanna. "Directions for the Management of Silkworms." Published posthumously in the *Philadelphia Medical and Physical Journal* (1804): 103–107.

Wulf, Karin. "'My Dear Liberty': Quaker Spinsterhood and Female Autonomy in

Eighteenth-Century Pennsylvania," in *Women and Freedom in Early America*, ed. Larry D. Eldridge. New York: New York University Press, 1997.

MASTER'S THESIS

Hunsberger, Barbara. "An Analysis of the Public Life of Susanna Wright." Master's thesis, Penn State University, 1982.

Image Credits

Page 4: Courtesy of Tate Images. Page 5: Courtesy of the Essex Record Office. Page 6: Courtesy of Haverford College, Quaker and Special Collections. Page 7 (top): Public domain. Page 7 (bottom): Library of Congress. Page 8: Courtesy of Haverford College, Quaker and Special Collections. Page 9 (top): Library of Congress. Page 9 (bottom): Courtesy of the Pennsylvania Academy of the Fine Arts. Page 10 (top): Courtesy of the Capitol Preservation Committee, Harrisburg, PA. Page 11: Historical Society of Pennsylvania. Page 12: Historical Society of Pennsylvania. Page 14: Courtesy of Haverford College, Quaker and Special Collections. Page 16: Courtesy of the Columbia Historic Preservation Society, Columbia, PA. Page 17 (top): Library of Congress. Page 17 (bottom): Courtesy of the Columbia Historic Preservation Society, Columbia, PA. Page 18: Library of Congress. Page 19: Author's collection. Page 20: Author's collection. Photographed with permission from the Landis Valley Village & Farm Museum. Page 21: Author's collection. Photographed with permission from the Landis Valley Village & Farm Museum. Page 22: Courtesy of the Pennsylvania State Archives. Page 24: Courtesy of the Metropolitan Museum of Art, Online Collection. Page 25: Virginia Miscellany Legal Papers, 1657-1791, Private Papers Collection, Library of Virginia (Accession 24715). Page 27: Author's collection. Page 31: Historical Society of Pennsylvania. Page 33: National Gallery of Art. Page 35 (left): Library of Congress. Page 35 (right): Courtesy of the Metropolitan Museum of Art. Page 36: Courtesy of Cerebro. Page 37: Courtesy of Yale University. Page 38: Courtesy of the Columbia Historic Preservation Society, Columbia, PA. Page 39: Courtesy of the New York Public Library. Page 40: Shutterstock, Inc. Page 45: Library Company of Philadelphia. Page 46: Courtesy of Haverford College, Quaker and Special Collections. Page 47: Library of Congress. Page 49: Historical Society of Pennsylvania. Page 51: Library of Congress. Page 52: Wikimedia Commons. Page 53 (top): Haverford College Library, Quaker Collection, Friends Freedman's Association, Collection no. 950. Page 53 (bottom): Library of Congress.

Acknowledgments

Special thanks to the many reference librarians, historical preservationists, and curators throughout Pennsylvania who aided my research: Willhem Echevarria at the Historical Society of Pennsylvania; Barry Rauhauser, staff curator and director of history on the Web, Lancaster Historical Society; Marjorie Bardeen, director of library services, LancasterHistory.org; Alicia De Miao at the University of Pennsylvania; and Grace Thiele, Haverford College Quaker and Special Collections. Special thanks to Ann Upton, curator of the Quaker Collection at Haverford College, who read a draft and offered valuable suggestions.

Warmest thanks to Suzanne Whallon at the Columbia Historic Preservation Society, who took an active interest in this book and went well beyond the call of duty in helping me locate documents and resolve discrepancies; Howard Reeves, editor beyond compare; the fabulously talented designer Maria Middleton; the meticulous managing editor Jen Graham; copyeditors Maxine Bartow and Leslie Kazanjian, who saved me from so many errors; Orlando Dos Reis, who helped with *everything*; and Andy, for the constant support and encouragement.

Index